years of being you

megha raina

INDIA · SINGAPORE · MALAYSIA

ISBN
Paperback 979-8-89498-389-9
Hardcase 979-8-89556-822-4

There is a story you have not heard, a story waiting for you to finish it.

Contents

LOVE

When dreams grow brighter with each sunset,
I light up my soul sitting next to you.

With every breath, a piece of you is woven into the fabric of my existence.

This muse of mine…

This muse of mine draws me to pages,
either to read or write,
enfolds me like mountains embrace a valley,
pulls me back like drops return to the sea,
warms me like a winter sunrise,
and sends chills down my spine like melting ice.
This muse of mine is a morning raga,
serene as a fully blossomed flower,
alive as earth feels after the first rain,
this muse of mine is a man in a child,
joyful and forever seeking more...

In the dance of chance and destiny, may our hearts recognize the melody.

You, My Love…

I often think of who I am in your absence
and what I become when you hold me close.
I praise God for your presence
and believe in devils when you leave.
With you, I find music in silence,
and when you say goodbye,
a guitar cannot put me at ease.

I am a book with your name on the first page,
anyone who reads it will know where I belong.
I am a fire burning for its wood,
and with your touch, my flames reach the sky,
I am a silent sea waiting for my moon,
my tides leap to whisper in your ears,
"I am yours."

I am the dance with you.
Without you, I cannot feel my feet.
I am the color of your clothes,
I become the road you walk on,
I turn into a sunset for your mind,
and then some water for your eyes.

I become the umbrella when it rains,
and sometimes the rain, for your touch.
I am the clay,
taking the shape you make,
I become the tree
offering you a little shade,
you will see me as a flower in your vase,
and a vase on your table.

In your presence, I change shapes and forms,
I burn, I melt, I become, and I reform.

16

You are the poetry my heart insists on writing.

The Fire and Desire

About to touch you, my flames soften,
for my desire is to reach deep into your bones,
to pour all my existence into yours,
to reveal who I am and what you have become,
a transformed man to the world, yet a child to me.

In your eyes, I see a million reasons to believe in magic.

The ease of living with you…

With every passing day, I believe that I have met you before.
I have held those hands and kissed you a million times,
I have known your body and nourished your soul.

I am sure I have lived many lifetimes with you.

Because what else can explain
this comfort with a stranger and
such beautiful convenience in chaos.
What else can be the reason for
my easy breathing when you are around and
such uncanny moments
that are impossible otherwise.

There is something in me that knows the inner you very well.

I wonder, will forever be long enough with you?

Magic…

I wish I could show you how it was.
There was a road,
as lost as your heart,
and clouds,
as messy as mine.
But together, it was magic,
Just like you and me.

Your presence in my life is nothing short of a miracle.

Love is the sculpture carved from the rawest emotions.
The artist can only be the heart.

The Sun and the Moon

The sun is a woman, and the moon is her lover.
How else could you explain their celestial dance?
She shines and offers herself every day,
while he bares his soul to her only twice a month.

How else do you explain a love like that?

24

Beneath the flesh, they saw the essence of each other's true being. In that vulnerable moment, the souls recognized each other.

October

After seasons of luring and longing,
lovers begin to shed their leaves of inhibition,
revealing the naked emotions of being human.
Two souls stand on rough patches,
with only vulnerability and truth between them.
Those green and rosy words transform
into moments of anger, jealousy, and shame.
Nothing remains hidden anymore.

This is when a true lover stands beside you,
holding your hand through the storm.
Only a real lover
embraces your darkest secrets,
accepts your fall,
stays close in the winter,
and then dances with you in the spring.

Fall is for real lovers…

When our hands meet, my universe aligns.

What Could Have Been...

Whenever I hear a beautiful love story,
I lose myself in dreams of what we might have been.
I start to weave your presence around me,
imagining you by my side in our living room,
carefully fixing my messy hair,
pulling me closer
to rest in your embrace,
as gracefully as the
sun sets on a silent lake.
I look into your eyes and
pick up the remote to
turn the music a little louder,
because I know
this is the moment
when your lips will meet mine.
A kiss that will always be a dream!

It is all in my mind, but it is so real.

28

I want to hold on to us and let our connection withstand everything.

Please, Will You?

Let us journey back to a time
when we were too young
to grasp the depths of love,
yet we gave it all we had.
Take me to those tender years
when our hands were soft,
yet our grip was so tight.

Let us return to that sweet phase
when "us" was all, we knew.
Run with me to those moments,
when we endured everything
silently
for
each other.
Let us again live the life of
happy sleepless nights
and the good mornings.

If you can not do any of this,
my darling,
just take me to the day
when we hugged last,
because this time,
I will not let you go.

I wonder what would have bloomed if I had asked you to stay?

You came and rewrote the script of my life,
turning everyday moments into extraordinary scenes.

Filled My Cup

I have wandered for a long time
with an unknown thirst called belongingness.
Across places and faces, I tried it all.
Ate, danced, spoke,
and stayed silent, too,
ran on beaches and
slept beneath the mountain's blue.

I did unspeakable and unimaginable,
yet no ocean quenched my thirst.
Then, on a dull day, our paths aligned,
and you offered me a drink
without asking.

I want you to know that
my life has shifted its course
from that fateful day.
I have been drinking
ever since you filled my cup.

You have become the only melody my heart dances to.

Sunshine and Moonlight in One...

There have been countless moments
when I have longed to express
the joy you bring into my life, and
how you fill my soul with happiness.
Each word you speak becomes a sign,
reminding me that life can be beautiful.
Your patience amidst the chaos reassures me
that despite all the challenges,
there is light at the end of the tunnel,
offering hope and healing.

Your forehead kisses are like sunshine,
and your warm hugs, moonlight in the dark.
Darling, on days like these,
I feel every ray touching us,
illuminating the longing
for a lifelong union.

If you are a dream, I do not wish to wake up!

Through loving you, I have discovered that love is the map shaping my journey.

Togetherness

I no longer wake up to your coffee kiss,
or to the warmth of our
shared cheese omelet bliss,
Without you, everything tastes of
loneliness and fading dreams.
The love songs no longer hold their charm,
and the sunset has lost its golden beams.

But I still read
your favorite books,
hoping to find
a memory in their hooks.
And as I turn each page,
I am reminded
of how beautiful
our togetherness was.

In separate worlds, we carry a shared heart.

The Rain We Drank...

And then, one day, it rained like never before.
You and I drenched in love,
unaware we were crafting memories,
we walked, sang, and danced in the rain…
the rainbow that evening was
a celebration of our love.

And now, look at us,
every time it rains,
we wait on roadsides
and close all the windows tight.
Not letting a drop touch our skin,
we choose to stay thirsty,
because
we both know…
no one can love us the way
we loved each other.

Cheers to the rain we drank together!

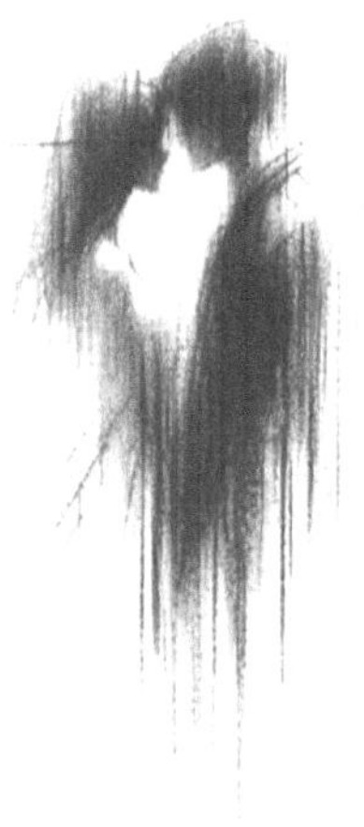

You are the "golden hour" of my sunset life.

How much of me do you carry?

Now that I am gone,
I watch you from far away,
as you smile and laugh,
busy with the rhythm of your days…
I wonder, my love,
how much of me do you still carry within?

Do you hear my laughter
in the echoes of your favorite song?
When you walk through familiar places,
do you feel my footsteps beside yours?
Or when you find yourself alone,
does the silence remind you
of our late-night talks and shared dreams?

Tell me, my love,
in the quiet moments between your laughter,
and the spaces between your breaths,
how much of me do you carry?

When was togetherness a physical thing?

I hope you wait,
and do not rush because it is late.
I hope you know the wait is worth it,
and you are worth the wait.

In my busy life, I pause -
feeling a tug, a gentle pull
towards a time when we were inseparable.
I feel your love like a warm embrace,
knowing time has not erased
the traces of what we once shared.

Your words linger within my heart,
like a cherished secret,
hidden but never forgotten.

A silent promise, forever true.

Together, we paint the sky with our laughter.

Becoming the Love, I was in

I am all you.
More you than you are.
It did not happen suddenly;
it was a slow process of becoming you.
Becoming the love, I was in.
Every morning, when I looked in the mirror,
I found you looking back at me and asking,
"How will you separate yourself from you?"

And the answer always was,
"I am all you.
More you than you are."

The sky got its rainbow,
Just like I got you,
Short-lived but complete.

Harmony in Differences

Lovely are the days when we sing the same song,
share secret jokes in public,
and walk the same path together.
It is delightful when our minds align,
enjoying the same books and thoughts.

But my favorite days are
when our stories diverge,
when I crave a party,
and you prefer to lounge in bed,
when we disagree on movie reviews,
when I want to watch a reality show,
and you want to stick to the news,
When I want a trip to the mountains
but you want to swim in the sea,
and when you order black coffee
instead of our usual green tea.

Our shared melodies and divergent tales make the echoes of us.
I love how we always make everything work.

The map of my soul is in your smiling eyes.

It Was You

That winter, when you first saw me in the pink sweater,
you said my cheeks turned pink, too.
It was not the dress; it was you.
Sitting across the table, sunlight on my face,
you looked at me as if you had found a treasure,
"What happened?" I asked, self-conscious,
"Your eyes are brown," you replied,
It was not the sunlight; it was you.
You reminded me of everything
I had forgotten about myself.
It was you.

It was always you.

Sometimes, he moves mountains for me,
and other times,
he does not shift to the other side of the bed.
I am in love with a man of moods.

Beyond Words…

My memories are fading away.
I sit and struggle to recall our firsts -
Our first kiss, birthday specials, movie nights.
I toss and turn, trying to remember
the moment you first said, "I love you."
but my mind draws a blank.
Sensing the chaos in my mind,
you hold my face in your hands,
and my heart starts to race.

A smile forms on my lips as I realize,
for even if the words escape me,
living with you always reminds me of the feeling.

In your touch, I have found a love that time cannot erase.

In you, I discovered the chapter my soul had been searching for.
I found the poem my dreams had whispered about.
You are what my heart always sought!

A soul-stirring love…

From the moment our eyes met first,
we knew this was no ordinary love,
it was an outrageous soul stirrer,
reminding us of a big void
we did not even know existed.
And from that day onward,
togetherness became our way of life.
We met daily.
We met even when we were apart,
for you never left me,
and I never left you.
Madly, deeply,
hopelessly in love!
We became one with each heartbeat.

And then our castle broke like it never existed!

My love for you is painted with the colors of eternity.

Tangled Hearts

Her love swept in like high-speed wind,
enveloping you from all sides,
sending chills down your spine,
shaking your notions of love,
notions of togetherness
beyond mere talking,
further than superficial touches.

Her love went deep within,
flowing like lifeblood
through your veins,
she knew your fear,
for she was scared, too.

But my darling, that is love.
Not just movies, coffee, or sex,
but the most cherished mess.

The journey is unpredictable yet endlessly beautiful.

In your every kiss on my forehead, I hear an unspoken vow.

A caesura

As he read that timeless Rumi verse,
with her hand soft and secure in his,
he altered the lines,
pausing to meet her gaze,
a moment of poetic grace,
a caesura,
With charm and sincerity, he said
"I love you."

And in that tender moment,
between verses and whispered words,
they found a new chapter unfolding,
where love spoke louder than any poem could.

As the sun sets, my sky is filled with colors of longing for you.

Echoes of Us

You and I may forget our love,
but do "they" remember?
The walls that whispered our secrets,
the roads that traced our journey,
the tables that echoed our laughter,
and the floors that carried our dance.

I wonder...
Do they keep our memories and
hold our universe within their embrace?

Our whispers are still heard in the whispers of the wind.

Come and wither my rust before I am gone.

Lovers of body, seekers of soul

There must be glitters that surround you,
but does the moonlight
grace your nights?
There must be fires, eager to dance,
but does your sun
shine warm on you?

You may have lovers
for your body's touch,
But is there someone
loving your soul, too?

Do you miss the one who truly loved you?

You are the answer to a question I did not know I asked.

In the quiet of the night,
your essence stays…

You are the melody I cherish,
the rhythm that guides my heart.
Your touch, it tingles my soul,
Come revive me before I am lost.
I have let go of all the shadows I once held,
You are the light that brightens my path.
Darling, you are the melody I cherish,
the rhythm that guides my heart.

With you, I have found the peace I always sought.

62

My heart is haunted by the echoes of your laughter.

Golden Hope

The secret is that I am hopeful.
Shamelessly hopeful of a day when
there will be no darkness to surround.
The earth will be bright with kindness.
Everyone,
standing peacefully
in their own light,
will throw
glitters of acceptance around.
Even the moon, glowing gold,
will see me walk to you,
and in that moment, so true,
I will softly say, "Yes, I do."

Amidst the stars, we will write our story on a full moon night.

The Real You…

I see you.
I see you always,
in the pages of a new book,
in the rustling of popcorn at a theater or
in the pressed buttons of an elevator.
I see you in the flicker of a candle's flame,
sitting beside me, holding my hand,
even in crowded parties where I feel alone,
or when I am making a heart on the beach sand.
I discover you in a random line of a love song,
find you in bustling malls, markets, and stalls,
and yes, I cherish you, in
my fluffy Sunday omelet.
In everything I see,
I see you.
In the mirror, too,
I see you.
Yet, none of it compares to
Seeing the real you.

Missing someone is a curse!

The Patient Shore

You do not need to try hard,
just be present,
sit, listen, and retain,
like a shore watching the waves,
absorbing each rise and fall,
silently embracing the changes,
as they slowly reveal all,
one by one,
layer by layer,
Until one day,
The shore truly knows them.

You do not need to try hard,
You just need to be there.

In the quiet of your patience, love finds its way to grow.

In Quest of You…

Dear You (the one I am yet to meet)
I wonder where you are!
Have you fallen in love? Does she value you?
Or was your heart broken?
because I know, just as mine,
it would take mere moments
to shatter yours, too.

I wonder how you are!
After having a hearty meal,
do you go for long strolls?
Do dreams of a perfect life
weave through those streets,
and does it ever make you
think of my existence?

If so, why haven't our paths crossed?
It keeps troubling me that time is slipping away,
the mirror hints at
wrinkles around my eyes.
I wonder,
will you still recognize
the sparkle in my eyes
born from the thoughts of You.

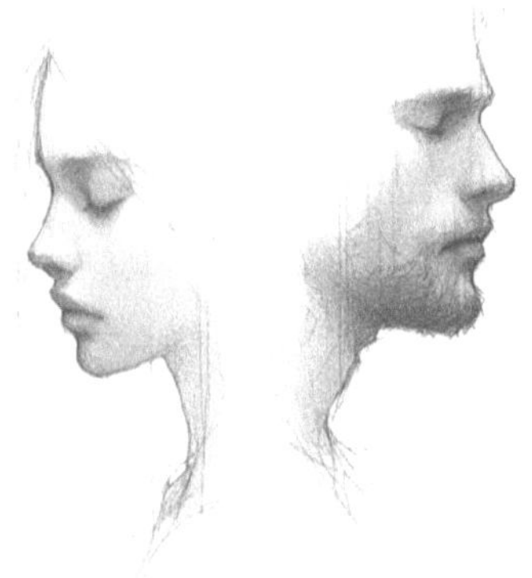

Unmasked

I want to know the emotions masked by your smile,
Show me the confusion lingering behind your clarity,
Tell me what made you cry
before you decided to put that mascara on,
Reveal the mess beneath this ironed shirt,
I long for the essence behind your expensive perfume,
Write to me about your first heartbreak,
that worst night and every failure you encountered.
Share what was lost in the quest for happiness,
Remind me why you could not speak up
when it was needed the most.
Tell me who you are beneath this naked body!
Let your guilt, regrets, and dark secrets be the main course,
and then let us move on to your
desires for the dessert we share.

I want to uncover the beauty of imperfection within you.

PAIN

75

Within me, a storm of hurt rages silently.

Home is a question that echoes unanswered in the hearts of refugees.

The answer that night!

I was ten when I heard this.
A man asked my father,
"So, when are you going back to your home?"
Papa took a breath and spoke long paragraphs,
I was too young to remember the words,
but I cannot forget how he cried that night.
It is carved in my heart because
he still does not have an answer to that.

And now when I know about my home
and homeland,
I wonder about the words he used that night,
the long paragraphs that helplessly said,
"I don't know."

Kashmir,
a paradise where
mountains hold untold tales of loss,
and greenery conceals the silent grief.

Kashmir

These beautiful mountains and trees,
stand and mourn the graves within them.
The grass is moist with the blood of lost children,
and the air still carries the smoke of burned homes.
Rustic buildings are formed from bodies
that were never returned to their families.
Few lotuses on Dal Lake resemble the faces
that will never see them again.

I am walking on earth's heaven, they say.
Kashmir.

Homeless

Among the names I have been called,
one echoed loud and clear,
"Homeless coward," they murmured,
igniting a silent fear.
For they overlooked the agony of
fleeing in the dead of night…

My father,
who left it all and chose to keep us alive,
do not call him a coward for not taking up guns,
do not call him shameless for seeking help,
because nobody chooses to be a refugee,
nobody desires to beg for food,
it is neither an identity,
nor a personality.
There are tears we drank,
there is pain we embraced,
and a havoc we managed.

Yes, we were homeless,
but not cowards,
and never hopeless.

Have you ever felt like a painting?
An art complete yet itching to reveal,
a story written well, yet misunderstood,
have you ever felt it, too?

Shrug It!

How long will you hold on?
To memories empty and cold,
broken promises and shattered truths,
to the clear abandonment,
and every piece of pain.
How long will you hold on
to the one that ripped you.
Shrug it all off.

Sometimes, the moonlight of your love is lost in the eclipse of their self-absorption.

The Failure

It was not you.
He was incapable of loving anyone.
Your face, a moonlight glow,
yet he could not see beyond scars.
Your body, home to a selfless soul,
ye he remained blind to your light.

It was not what you missed to do,
but what you did willingly, knowingly,
and out of love.
It was about the sacrifices you made,
sacrifices that are rarely seen in this world,
this busy and competitive world.

You said "yes" when you could have said "no."
and he took you for granted,
crushing you as he wanted.
It was your devotion to him
that left him doing nothing for you.
Assuming you would never leave,
he never tried to hold you.

Darling,
You loved him deeply enough to learn,
that love does not demand submission,
Love only surrenders.

It was not you. It was him.
He was incapable of love.

In the ashes of broken love, I wander, not yet ready to forgive the fire.

Forgive, maybe not!

I got an apology I did not seek,
and now I do not know what to do with it.
I am not ready yet,
not strong enough to forgive,
I am still looking for my pieces,
collecting the ashes of me, you left behind,
searching for myself in the places
where you left me alone,
wandering on streets that echo my loneliness…

This happened because,
I chose to wait.
I chose to believe.
I chose to love.
And you,
You chose to move on.

So, not yet,
I am not strong.
Not ready
to forgive you for breaking me,
Maybe one day,
when I stand tall again, I will think about your sorry,
and that day,
I could choose to forgive you, or maybe not.

When love broke me,
I feared I would be lost forever.
But I found myself in everything that is demolished.

Two halves of my heart

In a moment, my darling,
You split my heart in two,
and I carry these two parts inside.
One part, no one can heal,
and the other part is curing itself.
One weeps in silence
haunted by the past,
The other dreams softly
of a love that will last.

One carries the ache; the other holds hope!

I stay awake the whole night, mourning a few dreams that slipped through my grasp.

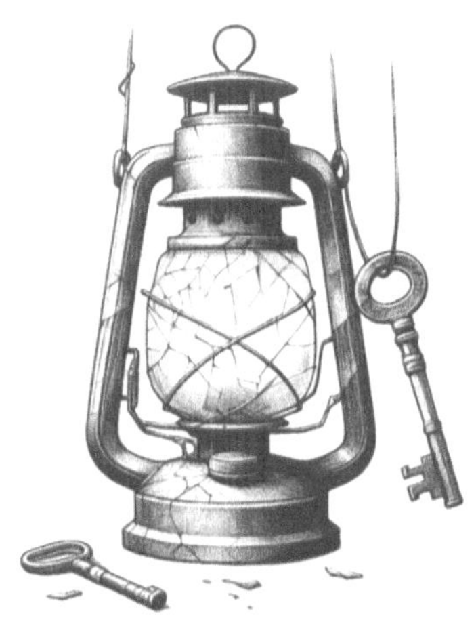

Dreams and Dawn

In the middle of the night
my vision is blurred by the tears,
as I am haunted by a dream
of you kissing someone else.
I turn and glance at the man
sleeping beside me,
and I imagine,
shaking and waking him up,
screaming and asking,
"What dreams possess you now?"

Instead, I sip water,
and I write,
until the dawn breaks and
I have bled tears on paper.

Each word is a testament to the tears that stain my soul…

True liberation comes from forgiving the self that once bowed to pain.

Healing from Within

Remember the times you felt sorry,
Sorry for making him angry,
for his abuse and misuse,
for slapping your face twice,
but your soul a million times.

Remember the times you felt sorry,
Because you went to a hobby class,
or invited your friends home,
or wore that favorite black dress,
or let your hair loose on the dance floor.
Remember how you cried for forgiveness,
and endured the bruises repeatedly.

Darling, listen closely -
you must say goodbye to your old self.
Because you do not need to say sorry to anyone
for living your life,
and if you want to,
you must say sorry to yourself
for not living and laughing enough.
You need to ask your soul for forgiveness
for the pain you allowed.

I looked at our old pictures today,
and I can see it all so clearly now,
my emotions, my hope, my soul,
everything was being murdered.

I have lived you a thousand times in my mind,
writing and rewriting our tale,
hoping for a different end,
yet every time the pages turn,
you break instead of mend.
No matter how our story begins,
You always end up as the abuser.

And she remained stuck between "being treated well" and "believing that he's sorry."

I often catch myself saying, "But it is how it is, and that's okay," while inside, I know nothing is okay. Deep down, my nerves write it in my blood, urging me to burn this expectation of being okay until it is gone forever.
This forced feeling of "being okay when we are not"
does not even deserve a grave,
Because from that soil,
a tree may grow,
burdened with expectations to conform,
to accept everything that comes its way,
In the name of traditions and morals
and an unsaid rule, this
tree must bear fruit and offer shade.

I knew 'enough' ended long ago,
yet like everyone else,
I wonder why I silenced that 15-year-old.
Why did I silence the girl who was strong enough
to be vulnerable in front of everyone?

I am going to let her rediscover her voice, free from any false expectations.

Your absence taught me the art of letting go, even when it hurts.

Will it be trivial things every day
or the weight of memories all at once?
Will it unfold gently, like a slow dance,
or strike swiftly, like a sudden storm?
I wonder, my darling,
how do you intend to erase me?

Perhaps you will rewrite our story,
painting over the hurt with new colors.
Tell me,
will you bury me beneath new smiles
or let the pain linger in unspoken words?
I ask, my darling,
How do you plan to forget me?

I knew it was self-destruction,
yet I savored every drop of sweet poison offered by your hands.

A part of me often wakes up from its ashes,
the ruined layer of my heart yearns to burn,
I want to invite trouble and let it finish me,
for what is it to live if I am not hurt enough?
I want to stare into the devil's eyes and let it possess me.

A prisoner of my own destruction,
a hostage of my own ruins,
standing here on the lava of my dead dreams,
I am a slow-burning candle but from both the ends.

Waiting for a bleak, painful end, I start believing in the darkness within me.

With every kiss, I danced closer to my own demise.

Youlessness

I have wandered often here,
in this zone of Youlessness,
"It's a different world," they say,
living away from your love.
You must know that here,
rain is just a weather change,
wine tastes like chilled water,
yet there is only a numbing ache,
as silent as my sleepless nights,
as cold as your final goodbye.

Each day is a struggle to find the light.

In your eyes, I saw the reflection of my downfall.
I fell willingly.

In my innocence…

Your love and a fire always surrounded me,
and both the natures remained a mystery.
In my innocence, I thought
you loved and hurt me,
at extremes.
While I embraced your highs and lows,
your expectation was calmness, I suppose.
You wanted me to remain naive, to stay green,
but my soul had limits, too,
slowly, it dried up and
I fell like autumn leaves.
My pain was unseen by you,
and your blame never ceased.
First the fire made me warm,
then hot, and
finally, it consumed me.
I sobbed with every burn,
I cried for help
as every part of me
was being scarred,
and then…
I could not.
I screamed out of anger!
And yelled, "Enough!"

My reaction to my burned self
was called a loud noise.
And my pain
was labeled as bad behavior.
In my innocence, I said, "I am sorry."

The distance between us is measured in the silent screams of my heart.

Silent Truths

The reasons
>for why we loved each other
>were so clear, so spoken,
>by our lips and our actions.

The reasons
>for why we unloved everything,
>were unspoken yet undeniable,
>written in our eyes and silence.

Our silence, louder than all words,
explained the painful recognition of our end.

Now, in the aftermath,
I search for reasons, for understanding,
but all I find is the echo of our silence.

Our touch, once electric, is now a ghostly reminder of intimacy.

In the void you left, my heart learned to speak the language of loss.

In your shoes…

I walked a few miles in your shoes,
They really hurt!
They are full of pain from the past,
they smell of broken trust and
are torn from bruises you carry inside.
With every step, I felt your sorrow,
the weight of burdens and blame,
each mile was a testament to your trials,
and your journey of despair and heartache.
Both sides are still tight because
you never gave space to your emotions,
and the sole is almost cracked because
you wouldn't let your soul heal.

May you find the space to breathe,
to heal your heart and mend your soul,
for even the most worn-out shoes
can walk a path towards being whole.

If love holds you and you feel the weight of unspoken desires, break free!

Bound by Love

It is never a strong grip on your neck,
it is a slow, soft suffocation,
enveloping you step by step, bit by bit,
taking your breath, with your permission.
It tastes sweet, smells enticing and looks special,
yet it is poison covered in affection.
Your friends will say it is love and care,
but you know, inside, it is "control".

In its embrace, you find comfort,
yet freedom slips through your fingers,
a delicate dance of shadows,
where love wears a mask of possession.

With each tender gesture, a chain forms,
binding you tighter to its will,
Until you realize,
that love should not suffocate,
but set your spirit free.

The love we once built now crumbles,
piece by piece,
entangled in unspoken truths
we can never unwind.

Roads that Whisper Pain

Every road in the early mornings,
fogs me with your memories.
I am reminded of
our togetherness, handheld walks,
life philosophy and our endless talks.
I hear myself ask, "What if I have to go away?"
You pull me close and say,
"I will follow you to the end of the earth,"
my heart smiles, and you continue,
"Until the earth has an end and a bend, you are mine!"
and then, as usual,
we laugh at the Flat Earth beliefs.

Today, I looked closer to see
how you made everything seem easy.
Call it my innocence or sheer stupidity,
I felt I was always going to be this happy.
Your ensuring words made me blush and
we laughed at everything under the sun,
little did I know, one day,
You would say the same words
to someone new,
and seeing tears in my eyes,
you both would laugh at me, too.

Silent Sufferings

I am sorry I was not ready to receive love.

You witnessed the worst version of me,
my broken, messed, and chaotic self,
I threw you in the fire every day, and yet,
you walked on eggshells for me.
I am sorry.
I look back at your silent suffering,
You paid for someone else's mistakes,
I avenged my pain on your innocence,
I offered storms to your tender heart,
yet you held on and endured it all.
I am sorry for not being kind to your soul.

Why are you waiting for them to say these words to you?
They will not.
And you do not need it. Find your peace.

Revisiting You!

Roaming in a castle of fake promises,
where beauty masks the shallowness within,
a place I entered as a hopeful girl,
only to depart
as a soul with many unseen scars.

I wander,
through corridors of illusions
where each step
is a reminder of trust misplaced.
Encountering lies and broken dreams,
I stand in front of you today, revisiting!

"Dear Girl, You Blindly Loved!"

I know I have come too far,
but what was I close to anyway?
I was merely living a life
that belonged to you.
My mornings, days, and nights
my words, love, and fights,
all shaped by your plans and moods.
I smiled, moved, and cried,
without a verse of my own,
I was simply dancing to your tune.

Now, as I reflect on you,
I scream at my old self,
for being so vulnerable,
so naive, so lost in you,
but then, a reply echoes back,
"Dear Girl, you blindly loved!"

Thank You for Being YOU

I know it might sound strange,
but I want to thank you,
for not only leaving me stranded,
but also, for the hurt you caused.
Thank you for your every action,
for what you did,
and what you did not do,
because without you,
I would not have known
such depths of sorrow,
or bled my heart onto paper
as if no eyes would read it,
I would never have
voiced my ache aloud…

Without you,
I would not have had the courage
to turn my pain into poetry.

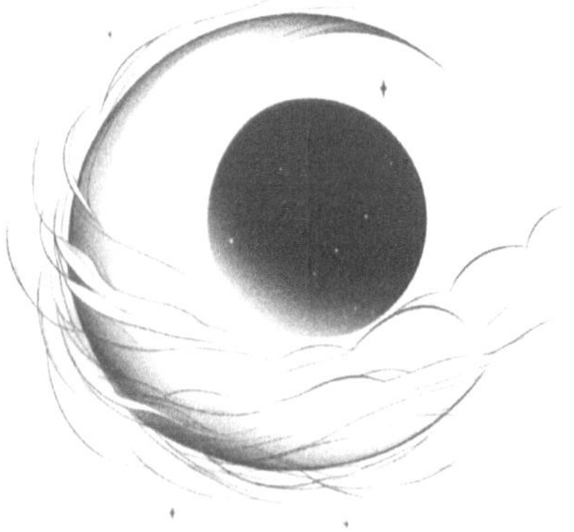

Life After You

Life is playing a new music,
smoke curls in darkness,
empty glasses everywhere,
and nothing seems familiar.
A million thoughts lie buried,
a thousand words remain unspoken,
Struggling earnestly,
Yet, failing to bridge,
This heart and these lips.

Suffocatingly Comfortable!

Today, I urge you to look inside,
deep into your core,
does it feel all right?
Or does concealing your true feelings
cause an ache within?
Are you content with this hidden truth
of who you truly are?
Or do you want to shatter
this façade, the image of "perfection?"

Because you know it within, that your truth,
in its rawness,
is your ultimate perfection,
while everything else
remains imperfect.

Peel away the layers of pretense.

LIFE

In the end, we all look back at a journey woven from realities and illusions.

When will my snow melt?

It is wintertime, and I patiently await,
for snow to uncover the leaves' fate,
to reveal their essence,
one true state,
and with thoughts untied, I ponder,
will I unveil my own hidden self?
When will my snow melt?

How sad is it when a symphony is silenced before its crescendo, such is the fate of a life not fully lived.

Art and its artist

In the act of creation,
an artist wants to picture
what others cannot…
So deeply and innocently
in love
with his craft,
he sees himself
as the creator.

Yet, in truth,
it is art that shapes the artist.

Art creates the artist.

A lover's return is a sunrise after a long night,
yet loneliness teaches profound lessons in patience.

Megha Raina

Lovers are not seasons

To whoever you are,

I know you are waiting for someone,
to show you spring's beauty,
and to ignite the summer's sun,
I see you watching the moon
like old times,
I feel your pain, your heavy heart,
I know it is tough to accept,
and it is breaking you inside.
But I must tell you this:
the one who left,
was meant to leave.
There is no use in waiting,
no anchor in this sea of hope,
So, open your eyes,
look at the leaves, rain, and sunshine.
Listen to the moon,
clearly whispering:
Seasons return
but lovers do not.

A seeker of serendipity and a nomad of imagination, finding poetry in every corner.

the life song

No, it does not end here.
My body must keep breathing,
The stage lights must stay on,
this sky yearns for clouds,
and earth awaits the rain.
My world refuses closure,
my song lingers, only halfway sung.

I am still writing the other half.

As the moon's glow guides me through the depths, I surrender to the dance of fate.

My Loopy Soul

Holding a fragile rope of twisted thread,
towing this boat of hope on a silent lake,
singing the songs of my lover,
"Warmth of sun on cold days,
light of the moon on darkest nights."

Will my wishes ever be heard by the tide?
Lead me to nothingness or the other side,
God, let these waves guide me today,
for the good I have done in my lifetime's play.

Wine swirling in a glass of forgotten silver,
Whirling and wasting, my loopy soul…

whirling and wasting, my loopy soul…

There are days when
my shadow hides my feelings, and
everything I do gets masked by the loudness of unspoken words.
Those days are for silent art.

For my readers

I will keep writing,
till each word bleeds,
and melts your heart,
I do not see any other way.

I want to write for you, pouring my endless soul into these verses.

When it all ends, I want to say that I lived in full color, true to my own shades.

Unburdened by time

Today, I plan to stop thinking about yesterday and tomorrow.
I will not even think about today's fleeting sorrow.
In this moment,
I shed all regrets of the past,
release my secret wishes
and stop dreaming about the perfect day!
I seek to feel nothing about you, them, or me,
I am clearing all memories
like a wiper cleans water
on the windshield, effortlessly.
Throwing away all emotions
like I shrug the snow off my boots.

Right now, I want to be nothing of what was, is or will be.
I just want to be.

We will talk about the rest later!

In this stillness, I find peace beyond yesterday and tomorrow.

Let go

And one day, it all fell into place.
Everything suddenly was so clear.
With all the clutter I had been through,
the confusion and tears,
those visible and invisible scars,
the suffering of my body and mind...
everything was gone like it never existed.
If only I had known it could be this simple,
how I wish someone had told me that
hurt could be released
by just letting it leave me.

I wish I had said to myself, "Let go."

Peace and clarity emerge from the aftermath of letting go.

The curious case of life

An unsolved mystery forever,
a tale tightly bound within,
Being everything in nothingness,
yet meaning nothing to everything,
crawling on countless spheres,
lost without a destination,
both the problem and the solution,
an enigma of existence,
This is a curious case of life.

Your poetry

The world has not been fair to you.
You have not been fair to many, too.
At times, you have wronged yourself,
and scratched your soul with a knife.
As you hurt and are hurting others,
I hope someday you pour
your heart onto paper.
Believe me,
what you write will transform into poetry.
Your poetry. It is that simple.

In each verse, your heart's melody becomes the poetry of your journey.

Seek answers inside.
No one knows you deeper than you do.

I am this and that

This innocent child who shares with a stranger,
That worldly woman who knows how to claim her dues,
This lover, believing in togetherness and forever,
That nomad who never thinks about tomorrow…

This free spirit, dancing and celebrating life,
That peaceful soul who drinks in solitude…

I am this and that.

I am all of this and more.
In the kaleidoscope of me, there is a universe to explore.

To someone who gave me a drop of their presence when I was thirsty,
my ocean of existence will always be yours.

Magic of hope

A little birdie whispered to me,
there is brightness ahead,
With surprises aplenty,
endless love and
peaceful nights.
For you, for me, and
for all who believe.

A new place

Wish I could explain you
the freedom I feel
in getting lost in a new place,
Wish I could show you
the liberation of losing everything
I thought I had to keep mine.
I have let go of the baggage of expectations,
and forgiven me
for all the decisions I took or did not take,
for all the pain I endured or pushed back,
and now, I feel free,
from everyone and
from my old self.

A bird in its flight is free from home, too.

A traveler's life is lost on the map and found on the journey.

Travel to know yourself

As I immerse myself in new cultures,
walk unfamiliar paths,
savor new flavors,
and converse with people far from home,
this newness reflects a part of me,
waiting to be explored,
waiting to be known,
and unique in itself!

Travel. Travel more. Travel often!

Do you?

You crossed rivers of hard work,
learned all the tricks of the trade,
put on the mask, made new friends,
and left behind those who slowed you down.
You lost a little peace and gained ego,
ran as fast as you could
and reached the top.
You are almost who you want to be.
Look at yourself and tell me one thing:
Do you like it here,
or do you want to return
to the person you were?

Which version of you was better?

Wish the only things we carried from yesterday to tomorrow were the lessons learned.

Unfortunately, what we carry more is the pain of learning those lessons.

The days that remain a mystery…

Sometimes, I hold back from writing,
for I am afraid the words will know
how much I burn,
how deeply I crave,
and why I turn to them each day.
I do not want these small letters to understand
how they calm my chaos,
nurture my imagination,
or how these syllables carry me gently,
like a breeze through my hair on a sunset-kissed lake.

Within the ink, my soul takes flight!

Mother is a sanctuary of unconditional love.
A compass that will always guide you back home.

Mother

Mother, how I wonder
about our connection.
There are days I see us as the same,
and no matter what happens,
I know you are my love,
and I am yours.
But then there are moments
when I realize
we are not the same at all.
We are so different,
because you can be me,
but I can never be YOU.

You are the reason I believe in selfless love!

Lost time is a ghost haunting you with "could have" moments.

Maybe…

Just like so many other things,
this was left unfinished.
A story lingering on the edge of lips,
waiting for a dawn that never breaks.
Just like so many times,
I said,
"Maybe some other time."

I wish all your emotions get an outlet.
Because in every "some other time,"
a piece of us is lost
to the ever-ticking clock.

It is soon going to be over...

Embrace this wonderful maze
as you would a compliment,
with humility.
Welcome the chaos
as you would a friend,
with a smile.
Tread these thorns
as you would walk in heels,
with grace.
It may not be your best moment,
but remember who you are.
Don't you know who you are?

Don't you know who you are?

Rise with every morning,
for in your heart lies the strength of the sun.
Cherish each step,
for even in shadows, you are the light.

The pros and cons of living fully

While I enjoy the beach breeze,
tiny sand particles sting my eyes,
my feet feel relaxed yet dirty in the sand.
My mind savors the sights
yet remains aware of the fleeting present.
I cherish this solitude, but
loneliness shakes my hand sometimes.
The sun kisses my skin,
leaving traces of its warmth,
I let my hair flow freely, knowing
it will become wild and messy.

For every moment of bliss,
there is a whisper of sorrow,
every joy has a price to pay,
and we must accept it.

Happy and sad can exist together.

Within every smile, a tear lingers…
within every tear, a smile hides.

Somewhere, we are all the same

We are all diluted
by what we do
or
by what happens to us.
We are all abandoned,
by someone else,
or by ourselves.
We are all broken,
by promises we keep,
or the ones we break.

I have moved on from your loss,
because it was never mine.
How could I lose what I never had?

It is too late now.
I have traveled beyond where I intended,
so far that even if I turn back,
no one is there waiting for me.
So, I stand here,
unsure if I should continue walking,
and if so,
which direction to take…

In my ignorance, sometimes I want the path to seek me.

Conveniently Complex and Comfortably Chaotic.

It Really Is Time...

I know you have done unspeakable things,
and your past is someone you would rather forget.
I am aware of your many sins,
but I also know
you have survived loneliness and distress,
endured a journey filled with
experiences and regrets.
Now, my dear, it is time
to stop drowning in guilty gulps of wine.
Now, my dear, it is time
to start anew and shine.

You just need to be who you want to be...

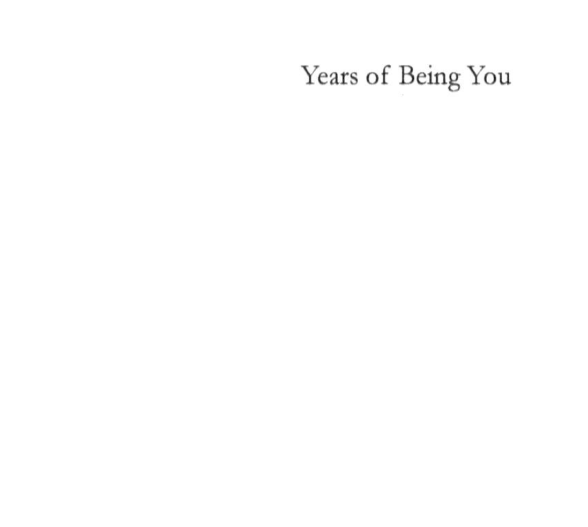

From the ashes of what was, the phoenix of what could be rises.

For as long as I can remember

I have been afraid for as long as I can remember,
spinning around known and unknown fears,
biting my nails, with a crumpled brow,
never recognizing my invisible crown,
afraid of my wings and my flight,
always terrified of crashing to the ground.

My lips stayed silent, my heart sank,
and I struggled to talk,
there was permanently a heavy-weight
pressed on my chest.
My legs and feet were fine,
but when needed, I could not walk.

I searched for others to lift me up,
I cried for comfort, screamed for help,
until I realized the answer was not in fear,
the answer was in faith.
The answer was within me...

The answer was me.

After everything you have done,
I cannot bring myself to wish the same fate for you,
Perhaps I loved you too deeply to wish harm,
But I do hope you never find someone like me,
I hope you are unable to hurt another soul again.
Rest, I will leave it to the universe to decide.

I will let fate do the maths.

Poetry is reality bleeding from a poet's heart.

I looked within and started writing; the ink never ran dry.

If only lived well…

Everything is transitory.
Happiness will leave you.
Sadness will go away.
Anger will subside.
Regret will fade.
Hatred will soften.

But love endures.
When lived fully, love is everlasting.

I am not from a country or a culture,
I belong to the world of words.

Life could have been simple, too.

You meet someone,
You like them with all your heart,
love them with all your soul,
they chose to hurt you,
but you stay strong and walk away.
You move on to a new life,
positive and happy once more.
If only it were this simple.

If only it were this simple…

Acknowledgement

To my beloved parents, your sacrifices have been the foundation upon which I have built my dreams. I am eternally grateful for your selfless love.

To my partner, your unwavering belief in my individuality has given me the courage to embark on unique paths. Thank you for being my anchor in this journey towards self expression and liberation.

Arzoo,

You are the brightest light in my life. May your dreams be boundless, and may you always find the strength within to follow your heart with grace and courage. I will always be by your side, no matter what.

To you, my reader,

As you close the final page of this book, my heart is filled with gratitude for the moments we have shared. Thank you for journeying alongside me through these pages. I hope the pages have given you moments of escape, solace and, perhaps, reflection.

Remember, our stories are intertwined.

As you step away from these words, may they continue to resonate in your heart, offering you refuge in times of need.

Thank you for embracing this journey with me. It is an honor to share this book with you.

Love,
Megha

www.ingramcontent.com/pod-product-compliance
Lightning Source LLC
Chambersburg PA
CBHW021357150726
47989CB00005B/2282